## Precious Time: Unlocking the Secrets of Productivity

Copyright © 2024 Reginaldo Osnildo
All rights reserved.

PRESENTATION

INTRODUCTION TO PRODUCTIVITY

UNDERSTANDING TIME

MULTITASKING MYTHOLOGY

SETTING CLEAR GOALS

EFFICIENT PRIORITIZATION

TIME MANAGEMENT TECHNIQUES

THE ROLE OF ROUTINE IN PRODUCTIVITY

TECHNOLOGY AND PRODUCTIVITY

MINIMIZING DISTRACTIONS

THE SCIENCE OF REST

FOOD AND PRODUCTIVITY

PHYSICAL EXERCISE AND MENTAL EFFICIENCY

MINDFULNESS AND FOCUS

OPTIMIZED WORK ENVIRONMENT

CONSTANT LEARNING AND GROWTH

RESILIENCE AND STRESS MANAGEMENT

TOOLS AND APPS FOR PRODUCTIVITY

DELEGATION AND TEAMWORK

THE POWER OF "NO"

PRODUCTIVITY AND LIFE BALANCE

EVALUATING YOUR PRODUCTIVITY

AVOIDING PROCRASTINATION

FINANCIAL PLANNING AND PRODUCTIVITY

FUTURE OF PRODUCTIVITY

CREATING YOUR PERSONAL PRODUCTIVITY FORMULA

INTEGRATING PRODUCTIVITY INTO LIFE

REGINALDO OSNILDO

# PRESENTATION

Welcome to " **Precious Time: Unlocking the Secrets of Productivity** ," a comprehensive guide designed to transform not just how you manage your hours, but how you live your life. This book is the result of in-depth research and personal experience, shaped to offer valuable insights, proven techniques and practical advice that will help you optimize your time and significantly increase your productivity.

Productivity is not just about getting more done in less time; It's about doing what's important, efficiently, so you can achieve your goals and have time for what really matters. In this book, we will cover everything from traditional methods to the most recent innovations in time management and efficiency, all with a fresh look and adapted to today's challenges and opportunities.

My intention is that by the time you turn the last page of this book, you will not only have accumulated knowledge, but will also be equipped with practical tools to apply in your everyday life. I'm bringing my perception to update the concepts of productivity and time management, synthesizing knowledge in a way that makes your life easier and contributes to your journey towards a more fulfilled and balanced existence.

Throughout the chapters, you will be guided through a journey of self-knowledge and discovery, learning to:

- Understand the essence of productivity and how to apply it in your daily life.

- Recognize the importance of time and how to use it to your advantage.

- Uncover the myths of multitasking and adopt more efficient practices.

- Establish clear and achievable goals, fundamental to your success.

- Prioritize tasks efficiently, maximizing your time and

effort.

- Integrate time management techniques that really work.

- And much more, from the role of technology to strategies to avoid procrastination, including the importance of rest and how to create an optimized work environment.

Each chapter is complete in itself, but is also part of a cohesive journey that builds your understanding and skills step by step. At the end of each chapter, I invite you to continue forward, as each new segment opens doors to further improve your efficiency and well-being.

This is more than a book; It is an invitation to rethink and remodel your relationship with time, work and personal life. Whether you are a student, a professional, an entrepreneur or someone looking for balance and fulfillment, this guide is for you.

So, I invite you to embark on this transformative journey. Let's uncover the secrets of productivity together and pave the way for a richer, more satisfying life. Are you ready to get started? The next chapter awaits you.

Yours sincerely

Reginaldo Osnildo

# INTRODUCTION TO PRODUCTIVITY

Productivity is a word that resonates in many aspects of our lives, being often associated with work and professional success. However, its true meaning goes far beyond that. Productivity is about achieving significant results efficiently, using our most limited resource well: time. It's about doing the right things, the right way, so that we can live our lives as fully and satisfyingly as possible.

## THE ESSENCE OF PRODUCTIVITY

Have you ever stopped to think about what it really means to be productive? It's not just about crossing items off a to-do list or being busy all day. Being productive is achieving goals that are important to you, in an intelligent and sustainable way. It's about being clear about your goals, prioritizing your actions and, above all, maintaining a balance between work, leisure and rest. In this chapter, we'll explore the essence of productivity and how you can apply it to transform your life.

## WHY DOES PRODUCTIVITY MATTER?

In a world that values speed and efficiency, learning to be productive is essential. However, the importance of productivity transcends the simple ability to do more in less time. It's about improving the quality of our work and our lives. When we are productive, we have more time for what truly matters to us, be it spending time with our family, dedicating ourselves to hobbies, studying or taking care of our health.

Plus, productivity helps us feel more fulfilled and less stressed because we know we're making the most of our time and resources. This not only improves our overall well-being, but also allows us to contribute more meaningfully to the world around us.

## DISCOVERING THE CONCEPT OF PRODUCTIVITY

Productivity is not a single concept, uniformly applicable to everyone. Each person has their own needs, goals and challenges.

So in this book, we'll approach productivity in a way that respects your individuality, helping you discover strategies that work for you.

We will explore proven techniques and methods, but always with a critical eye, adapting them to your reality. You will learn to recognize the productivity myths that may be hindering your progress and adopt practices that truly increase your efficiency and satisfaction.

Throughout this chapter, I hope you have begun to reflect on what productivity means to you and why it is so crucial in our quest for a full and fulfilled life. But this is just the beginning. In the next chapter, "**UNDERSTANDING TIME**", we will dive into different perceptions of time and how they affect our productivity.

Let's explore how our relationship with time can both propel us forward and hold us back, and how we can begin to see time as an ally, not an enemy. I invite you to continue this journey with us, as we together uncover the secrets to optimizing your time and taking your productivity to new heights.

Get ready to transform the way you think and act regarding time and productivity. The next chapter awaits you, full of insights and strategies that will change the way you live and work. Let's go ahead?

# UNDERSTANDING TIME

Time is a fascinating and complex concept, which influences all areas of our lives. Our perception of time can profoundly affect our productivity, well-being and, ultimately, our happiness. But what do we really mean by time? And how can we make it our ally in the search for a more productive and fulfilled life? This chapter dives into different perceptions of time and explores how they shape our lives and productivity.

## THE MULTIFACETED NATURE OF TIME

We often treat time as a fixed and limited resource, a straight line that runs out. However, time is much more than that. It is cyclical, as we observe in the seasons and cycles of nature, and it is relative, varying according to our activities, emotions and even cultures. This broader and more flexible understanding of time can help us use it more consciously and productively.

## CULTURAL PERCEPTIONS OF TIME

Different cultures have different perceptions of time, which can influence how we plan, act and prioritize our lives. While some cultures emphasize punctuality and a strict schedule, others value flexibility and the present moment. Recognizing and respecting these cultural differences is essential for effective communication and collaboration, especially in an increasingly globalized world.

## TIME AND PRODUCTIVITY

Our relationship with time directly affects our ability to be productive. Procrastination, for example, is a common challenge that reflects a struggle against time. On the other hand, the feeling of urgency can drive us to act, but it can also lead to stress and burnout. The key is to find a balance, using time effectively without overwhelming ourselves.

## MAKING TIME OUR ALLY

To make time our ally, we need to start seeing it as a flexible tool, not an implacable enemy. This means:

- **Accept the relative nature of time** : Recognize that our perception of time can change depending on what we are doing and how we are feeling.

- **Plan flexibly** : Allow space in our schedules for the unexpected and for rest, balancing structure with adaptability.

- **Prioritize the present** : Although it is important to plan for the future, living in the present allows us to appreciate and enjoy each moment, making us more aware and focused.

By better understanding time and our relationship with it, we can begin to transform our productivity and our lives. However, recognizing these concepts is just the beginning. In the next chapter, "**MULTITASKING MYTHOLOGY**", we will unravel one of the biggest myths of modern productivity and explore more effective alternatives for managing our time and tasks.

Get ready to challenge some of the most ingrained notions about work and efficiency. Let's together explore how more focused and intentional approaches can not only increase our productivity, but also improve our quality of life. Are you ready to continue this journey with us? The next chapter awaits with practical strategies and transformative insights. Let's go ahead!

# MULTITASKING MYTHOLOGY

In our never-ending quest for efficiency and productivity, many of us turn to multitasking as a seemingly ideal solution. The ability to multitask is often seen as a valuable skill in the modern workplace. However, what science and experience show us is quite different. This chapter will demystify the effectiveness of multitasking and present more productive alternatives that can transform the way you work and live.

## THE TRUTH ABOUT MULTITASKING

Contrary to popular belief, multitasking not only reduces our efficiency but can also lower the quality of our work. When we try to do several tasks at the same time, our brain is not actually processing everything simultaneously. Instead, he's quickly switching between tasks, which can lead to mental fatigue and mistakes.

## THE IMPACT OF MULTITASKING ON PRODUCTIVITY

Studies show that multitasking can reduce productivity by up to 40%. This is due to several factors, including the increase in time needed to complete tasks and the decrease in the quality of work. Additionally, multitasking can impair our ability to concentrate and focus in the long term, making it increasingly difficult to engage deeply in single tasks.

## ALTERNATIVES TO MULTITASKING

- **Monotasking Focus** : The key to replacing multitasking is to embrace monotasking - the practice of focusing on a single task at a time. This allows our brain to dedicate its full attention and resources to this task, increasing the efficiency and quality of our work.

- **Pomodoro Technique** : An effective strategy for improving focus and productivity is the Pomodoro Technique, which involves working with full concentration for periods of 25 minutes, followed by brief breaks. This technique helps maintain sharp focus and prevents fatigue.

- **Task prioritization** : Another method to combat the need to multitask is to learn how to effectively prioritize tasks. This involves identifying what is most important and urgent and focusing on those activities before moving on to lower priority tasks.

By recognizing the myths of multitasking and adopting more focused and intentional practices, you can significantly increase your productivity and improve the quality of your work and life. This chapter opened your eyes to the reality of multitasking and offered viable alternatives that can make a big difference in your daily life.

However, this is just the beginning. In the next chapter, "**SETTING CLEAR GOALS**," we'll explore how setting clear, achievable goals is crucial to improving productivity. Let's dive into techniques for setting effective goals that guide your actions and keep you on track for success.

Get ready to take the next step on your journey to becoming more productive. With well-defined goals, you will be able to focus your energy on the tasks that really matter and move forward in a more effective and satisfactory way. Are you ready to explore the power of clear goals? Let's move forward, as the next chapter awaits you with valuable insights and strategies to turn your dreams and projects into reality.

# SETTING CLEAR GOALS

Setting goals is one of the first steps towards any successful journey, including the search for productivity. However, it is not enough to just set goals; It is crucial that they are clear, achievable and motivating. This chapter will guide you through an effective goal-setting process, turning vague aspirations into concrete action plans that drive progress and efficiency.

## THE IMPORTANCE OF CLEAR GOALS

Clear goals serve as a beacon, guiding your actions and keeping you on track amid the distractions and challenges of everyday life. They provide focus, direction and a sense of purpose, as well as being essential for measuring progress and celebrating achievements. Without well-defined goals, it's easy to get lost in unimportant tasks or procrastinate.

## HOW TO SET EFFECTIVE GOALS

- **Be specific** : Generic goals tend to be less effective. Instead of "improving your health," opt for "walking 30 minutes every day." The more specific, the better.

- **Make them measurable** : Establish clear success criteria. Not only does this help you stay focused, but it also allows you to see progress and adjust the plan as needed.

- **Realistic Achievement** : While it's good to challenge yourself, your goals also need to be achievable. Setting unrealistic goals can lead to frustration and discouragement.

- **Relevance** : Your goals must be aligned with your values and long-term objectives. This increases motivation and the likelihood of success.

- **Set deadline** : Setting a deadline creates a sense of urgency and helps avoid procrastination. Make sure deadlines are realistic and flexible if necessary.

## THE SMART TECHNIQUE

A useful tool in goal setting is the SMART technique, which stands for Specific, Measurable, Achievable, Relevant and Timely. This approach helps you create a clear picture of what you want to achieve and how, making your goals more tangible and manageable.

By applying these principles to set clear goals, you will take a big step toward optimizing your productivity. Goals work like a map, directing your actions and helping you keep your focus on the tasks that truly matter.

Now that you understand the importance of setting clear goals and how to do so effectively, the next step is to learn how to prioritize those goals and tasks efficiently. In the next chapter, "**EFFICIENT PRIORITIZATION**," we'll explore methods for organizing your tasks so that you maximize your time and effort by focusing on the activities that generate the greatest impact.

Get ready to dive into strategies that will transform your ability to manage time, ensuring every action takes you closer to your goals. With the right tools and techniques, you'll be well-equipped to prioritize efficiently and make significant strides toward your goals. Let's move on to the next chapter together, where we will continue to pave the way for unprecedented productivity.

# EFFICIENT PRIORITIZATION

The art of prioritization is key to maximizing productivity and ensuring your time and energy are invested in the most important activities. With so many demands competing for our attention, learning to distinguish between the urgent and the important is more crucial than ever. This chapter is dedicated to exploring effective prioritization methods that can help you focus on the tasks that truly drive your progress and contribute significantly to your goals.

## THE EISENHOWER MATRIX

An extremely useful tool for efficient prioritization is the Eisenhower Matrix, which divides tasks into four categories based on their urgency and importance:

- **Important and urgent** : Tasks that need to be done immediately.

- **Important but not urgent** : Tasks that contribute to your long-term goals but do not have an imminent deadline.

- **Not important, but urgent** : Tasks that require immediate attention but do not contribute significantly to your goals.

- **Not important and not urgent** : Activities that do not contribute to your goals and do not have a specific deadline.

Focusing on "important but not urgent" tasks is key to moving towards your goals without falling into the trap of constant reactivity to "urgent" demands.

## DIFFERENTIATING URGENT FROM IMPORTANT

The ability to differentiate between urgent and important tasks is vital. We often end up dedicating most of our time to urgent tasks, neglecting those that are important for our personal and professional growth. Learning to identify and prioritize important tasks can lead to significant improvements in your productivity and well-being.

## TECHNIQUES FOR EFFICIENT PRIORITIZATION

- **Make a list** : Start the day or week with a list of tasks, classifying them according to the Eisenhower Matrix.

- **The two-minute rule** : If a task can be completed in two minutes or less, do it immediately. This helps you whittle down your to-do list quickly and stay focused on the most meaningful activities.

- **Time blocks** : Dedicate specific blocks of time to important tasks, ensuring they receive due attention without interruptions.

- **Regular review** : Review your priorities regularly to adjust to changing circumstances or goals. What was important yesterday may not be important today.

Mastering the art of prioritization is not just about getting more done; It's about doing what's right and doing it well. By applying these techniques, you'll be on your way to achieving remarkable efficiency, ensuring that each day is a meaningful step toward your goals.

Now that you're equipped with the tools you need to efficiently prioritize your tasks, you're ready to dive into specific time management techniques that can take your productivity to a new level. In the next chapter, "**TIME MANAGEMENT TECHNIQUES**," we'll explore proven strategies like the Pomodoro Technique and the GTD Method (Getting Things Done), which will help you optimize your time and energy, turning your goals into reality.

Get ready to deepen your time management knowledge and skills. With the right techniques, you will not only be able to do more, but also do better, leading a more fulfilled and balanced life. Let's move forward, towards a more productive and satisfying future.

# TIME MANAGEMENT TECHNIQUES

Mastering time management is essential for anyone who wants to be more productive, achieve their goals and have time for what really matters. This chapter will introduce you to proven time management techniques such as the Pomodoro Technique and the GTD Method ( Getting Things Done ), which can help you optimize your day and take your productivity to new heights.

## THE POMODORO TECHNIQUE

Created by Francesco Cirillo in the late 1980s, the Pomodoro Technique is a time management method that aims to increase your productivity by keeping your mind fresh and focused. The process is simple:

> 1 - Choose a task to be performed.
>
> 2 - Set a timer for 25 minutes and work on the task until the time runs out.
>
> 3 - Take a short 5-minute break.
>
> 4 - After every four "pomodoros", take a longer break of 15 to 30 minutes.

This technique helps you stay focused and avoid fatigue by ensuring regular periods of rest that rejuvenate your mental energy.

## THE GTD METHOD (GETTING THINGS DONE)

Developed by David Allen, GTD is a time management method that helps you organize and track your tasks and commitments. The GTD process is based on five essential steps:

> **1 - Capture** : Write down everything you need to do, whether on paper or digitally, to get it out of your mind and reduce stress.
>
> **2 – Clarify** : Process what you captured, deciding what is actionable and what is not. For actionable tasks, define the next required action.

**3 - Organize** : Put everything in the right place. Tasks should go to task lists, information to files, etc.

**4 - Reflect** : Regularly review your lists and systems to update them and decide on next actions.

**5 - Engage** : With everything organized and clear, choose your tasks with confidence and dedicate yourself to them.

Implementing GTD can be transformative because it allows you to clearly see what needs to be done and make an informed decision about what is most important to work on next.

**CUSTOMIZING YOUR APPROACH**

While the Pomodoro Technique and GTD are extremely effective, successful time management often requires a personalized approach. What works for one person may not be ideal for another. Try different techniques and adapt them to your specific needs, lifestyle and work preferences.

Mastering these techniques can transform the way you work and live, providing more fulfillment and less stress. By applying and adapting these methods to your lifestyle, you are taking an important step towards more efficient and sustainable productivity.

As we progress through this book, the next chapter, "**THE ROLE OF ROUTINE IN PRODUCTIVITY**," will explore how establishing daily routines can simplify your life, reduce procrastination, and maximize your efficiency. Well-structured routines can be the foundation on which you build a productive day and a fulfilling life.

Get ready to discover how small changes to your daily routine can have a profound impact on your overall productivity. Are you ready to transform your routines into powerful productivity tools? Let's move on and find out how.

# THE ROLE OF ROUTINE IN PRODUCTIVITY

Well-established routines are the foundation of a productive life. They create a structure that allows us to automate daily decisions, saving mental energy for tasks that require focus and creativity. This chapter explores how developing routines can increase your efficiency, reduce wasted time, and help you maintain a healthy work-life balance.

## THE IMPORTANCE OF ROUTINES

Routines are sequences of regular actions that make it easier to achieve our daily tasks and long-term goals. They help us:

- **Minimize procrastination** : By having an established routine, we reduce the barriers to getting started, as we know exactly what needs to be done.

- **Improve focus** : Routines eliminate the need to make constant decisions about what to do next, allowing us to direct our energy toward important tasks.

- **Increase efficiency** : Practice makes perfect. The more we perform a task within a routine, the faster and more efficient we become at it.

- **Strengthen healthy habits** : Incorporating exercise, meditation and other beneficial practices into our daily routine promotes overall well-being.

## HOW TO ESTABLISH PRODUCTIVE ROUTINES

- **Identify your priorities** : Determine which activities are essential to achieving your goals and incorporate them into your routine.

- **Start small** : Introduce new activities gradually. Try not to overload your routine with too many changes at once.

- **Be consistent** : Perform your routines at the same times whenever possible. Consistency reinforces habits.

- **Adjust as needed** : Your routine should suit your needs. If something isn't working, make adjustments.

- **Celebrate successes** : Recognize and celebrate when a new routine starts to feel natural. This reinforces positive behavior.

## BALANCING FLEXIBILITY AND STRUCTURE

While routines are fundamental to productivity, it is equally important to maintain a certain amount of flexibility. Unexpected situations will happen, and your ability to adapt your routine as needed is crucial to maintaining balance and avoiding stress.

By building and improving your routines, you create a clearer, less resistant path to achieving your goals. Established routines are like rails that guide your day, allowing you to move with purpose and efficiency.

The next chapter, **"TECHNOLOGY AND PRODUCTIVITY,"** will explore how technology can be both a tool and a hindrance to productivity. Let's discover together how to balance the use of technology to benefit, not harm, our efficiency and well-being. Are you ready to dive into the world of production technology? Keep moving forward, as there is much more to explore on the journey to optimize your time and increase your productivity.

# TECHNOLOGY AND PRODUCTIVITY

In an era dominated by technology, it is vital to understand how to use it to our advantage. Although technology can significantly increase our productivity, if not used wisely, it can also become a source of distractions and information overload. This chapter will cover how we can leverage technology to improve our efficiency, while avoiding the pitfalls that can compromise our performance.

## TECHNOLOGY AS A PRODUCTIVITY TOOL

Technology offers countless tools and applications designed to improve productivity. These are some examples:

- **Task management apps** : Tools like Todoist , Trello , and Asana can help organize your tasks and projects, making it easier to track progress and collaborate with others.

- **Distraction blockers** : Apps like Freedom and Cold Turkey let you temporarily block distracting websites and apps, helping you stay focused.

- **Automation technology** : Tools like IFTTT ( If This Then That ) and Zapier can automate repetitive tasks, saving you time and effort.

## FINDING THE BALANCE

While technology offers many benefits, it is crucial to strike a balance between connectivity and productivity. Here are some strategies for achieving that balance:

- **Set limits** : Set specific times of the day to check emails and social media, preventing these activities from dominating your time.

- **Smart notifications** : Adjust notification settings on your devices to only receive important alerts, reducing interruptions.

- **Conscious disconnection** : Set aside moments of the day or week to completely disconnect from technology, allowing your mind to rest and recharge.

## TECHNOLOGY AND THE CHALLENGE OF INFORMATION OVERLOAD

One of the biggest challenges of the digital age is information overload. To combat it:

- **Practice digital curation** : Be selective about the sources of information you choose to follow. This helps to reduce the volume of information to be processed.

- **Learn to take breaks** : Taking regular breaks from consuming digital information can prevent mental fatigue and improve concentration.

Technology, when used correctly, can be a powerful ally on your journey to becoming more productive. However, it is important to remember that true efficiency comes from the conscious and balanced use of these tools.

The next chapter, "**MINIMIZING DISTRACTIONS**", will delve into strategies for identifying and reducing distractions in your work and study environment, allowing you to maintain a high level of focus and productivity. Ready to learn how to master your environment and keep distractions at bay? Let's move forward, as each step takes us closer to a productive and fulfilled life.

# MINIMIZING DISTRACTIONS

Distractions are one of the biggest obstacles to productivity. In today's world where constant smartphone notifications and multiple browser tabs have become the norm, finding focus can feel like a constant battle. This chapter is dedicated to effective strategies for identifying and minimizing distractions, helping you maintain concentration and increase your efficiency.

## IDENTIFYING YOUR MAIN DISTRACTIONS

The first step to minimizing distractions is to identify them. Keep a journal for a few days to notice what often takes your attention away from work or studies. These distractions can range from constantly checking your smartphone to interruptions from colleagues or family.

## STRATEGIES TO MINIMIZE DISTRACTIONS

- **Create an appropriate work environment** : Organize your workspace to minimize visual and sound distractions. This might mean wearing noise-canceling headphones, keeping a tidy desk, or working in a secluded place if possible.

- **Manage your use of technology** : Make use of website and social media blocking applications during work or study hours. Establish specific periods of the day to check emails and messages, avoiding constant checking.

- **Set boundaries with others** : Communicate clearly with coworkers, friends, and family about your focused work hours, asking them to respect those times. Considering creating visual cues, such as a closed door or a warning, can help convey the need to focus.

- **Practice monotasking** : Commit to carrying out one task at a time. Close programs, tabs, and applications unrelated to the work at hand to avoid the temptation to switch tasks.

- **Use time management techniques** : Methods such as the Pomodoro Technique can help you maintain focus, alternating periods of intensive work with brief rest breaks.

## THE POWER OF HABITS

Developing the habit of minimizing distractions takes practice and patience. Start by implementing small changes and gradually increase your level of discipline. Celebrating small successes along the way can serve as motivation to keep up the effort.

By adopting these strategies to minimize distractions, you'll take a big step toward more effective productivity and deeper focus. The ability to maintain concentration despite the constant temptations of modern distractions is a powerful skill that can transform your efficiency and satisfaction in work and studies.

In the next chapter, "**THE SCIENCE OF REST**," we'll explore how adequate rest, including quality sleep and strategic breaks, is crucial for sustainable productivity. Ready to discover how to balance work and rest to achieve your goals without depleting your energy? Let's move on, because the balance between effort and recovery is the key to a productive and rewarding life.

# THE SCIENCE OF REST

Rest is a crucial component of productivity that is often underestimated. Long working hours and the cult of constant busyness can lead to burnout, reducing the quality of our work and affecting our physical and mental health. This chapter addresses the importance of adequate rest, including quality sleep and strategic breaks during the day, to maintain sustainable productivity and a balanced life.

## THE FUNDAMENTAL ROLE OF SLEEP

Sleep is not just a break in our day; it is an active state during which our body and mind undergo essential repair and strengthening processes. Lack of sleep can seriously impair our ability to concentrate, be creative and make decisions. To ensure restful sleep:

- **Maintain a regular sleep routine** : Going to bed and waking up at the same times helps regulate your body's biological clock.

- **Create an appropriate sleep environment** : Make sure your room is dark, quiet and at a comfortable temperature.

- **Unplug before bed** : Avoid screens and electronic devices at least an hour before bed to minimize exposure to blue light, which can disrupt your sleep cycle.

## THE IMPORTANCE OF PAUSES

In addition to nighttime sleep, short, regular breaks throughout the day are essential to maintain energy and focus. These breaks allow our mind to rest, reducing mental and physical fatigue. Some strategies include:

- **Pomodoro Technique** : Work for 25 minutes straight and then take a 5-minute break. Repeat the cycle throughout the day.

- **Active breaks** : Stand up, stretch or take a short walk to revitalize your body and mind.

- **Meditation and breathing** : Brief meditation practices or breathing exercises can help reduce stress and improve concentration.

## BALANCING WORK AND REST

Finding the right balance between work and rest is key to avoiding burnout and promoting healthy productivity. This balance can vary from person to person, so it's important to listen to your body and adjust your routines as needed.

By integrating adequate rest into your life, you will not only improve your productivity, but also your overall health and well-being. Remember that resting is not synonymous with wasted time; It's an investment in your ability to work more efficiently and creatively.

In the next chapter, "**FOOD AND PRODUCTIVITY**," we'll explore how our diet affects our energy and efficiency throughout the day. Ready to learn how nourishing your body can be a key to unlocking even greater levels of productivity? Let's move forward, fueling not only our bodies, but also our minds and spirits, for truly sustainable productivity.

# FOOD AND PRODUCTIVITY

The connection between food and productivity is profound, yet often underestimated. What we choose to consume has a direct impact not only on our physical health, but also on our mental capacity, energy levels and, consequently, our efficiency throughout the day. This chapter is dedicated to exploring how a balanced diet can fuel the body and mind, improving productivity and promoting overall well-being.

## THE IMPACT OF FOOD ON PRODUCTIVITY

Proper nutrition provides the body with the nutrients it needs to function optimally. A poor diet, on the other hand, can lead to fatigue, decreased concentration, and eventually health problems that negatively affect productivity. Let's examine how we can optimize our nutrition to support our performance.

## BASIC PRINCIPLES OF A PRODUCTIVE DIET

- **Nutritional balance** : Include a variety of foods in your diet to ensure a good mix of carbohydrates, proteins, fats, vitamins and minerals. Each of these nutrients plays a crucial role in supporting energy and cognitive function.

- **Hydration** : Staying adequately hydrated is essential for productivity. Dehydration can lead to a feeling of fatigue and decreased ability to concentrate.

- **Regular eating breaks** : Skipping meals can result in a drop in blood sugar levels, affecting your energy and concentration. Eating at regular intervals helps maintain stable energy throughout the day.

- **Limit sugars and caffeine** : While sugar and caffeine can offer a temporary boost of energy, they can lead to spikes and crashes, negatively affecting your long-term productivity . Opt for sustainable energy sources like whole grains and fruits.

## TIPS FOR INTEGRATING HEALTHY EATING INTO YOUR DAILY

## ROUTINE

- **Meal prep** : Take time to plan and prepare your meals and snacks in advance. This can help you avoid impulsive and less healthy food choices.

- **Smart snacks** : Keep healthy snacks nearby, like fruit, nuts and yogurt, to combat hunger without turning to less nutritious options.

- **Listen to your body** : Pay attention to your body's signals. Eating too much or too little can affect your energy and focus. Learn to recognize when you are truly hungry versus when you are eating out of boredom or stress.

By nourishing your body with the right foods, you will be equipped to not only face your daily challenges with renewed energy, but also maintain long-term health that supports a productive and fulfilling life.

Next chapter, "**PHYSICAL EXERCISE AND MENTAL EFFICIENCY**", we will delve into the symbiotic relationship between regular physical activity and mental performance. Ready to discover how movement can be a powerful ally in your quest for productivity? Let's move forward, as the integration of body and mental care is essential to achieve excellence in all aspects of life.

# PHYSICAL EXERCISE AND MENTAL EFFICIENCY

The connection between physical exercise and mental efficiency is undeniable and increasingly supported by scientific research. Regular physical activity not only benefits the body, it also has a profound impact on our cognitive ability, creativity, stress levels and productivity. This chapter discusses how integrating exercise into your routine can significantly improve your mental and emotional performance, boosting your efficiency in all areas of life.

## THE IMPACT OF EXERCISE ON THE MIND

Exercising regularly can lead to notable improvements in brain function, including:

- **Improved memory and concentration** : Exercise increases blood flow to the brain, which can help improve cognitive function and protect memory.

- **Reduction of stress and anxiety** : Physical activity releases endorphins, chemicals in the brain that act as natural painkillers and improve the ability to sleep, which reduces stress.

- **Increased creativity** : Exercise, especially outdoor exercise, can stimulate creativity by offering an escape from daily routines and providing new perspectives.

## INCORPORATING EXERCISE INTO YOUR ROUTINE

Integrating physical activity into your daily routine doesn't have to be a chore. Here are some tips to get started:

- **Choose activities you enjoy** : You're more likely to maintain an exercise routine if you're doing something you enjoy. Try different activities until you find one or more that you like.

- **Set realistic goals** : Start with small, achievable goals and gradually increase the intensity and duration of exercise as your fitness improves.

**- Integrate exercise into your daily life** : Instead of viewing exercise as an additional chore, find ways to incorporate more physical activity into your regular routine, such as walking during phone calls or opting for stairs instead of the elevator.

**- Create a regular exercise routine** : Establish fixed times to exercise. This helps turn exercise into a habit and ensures it fits into your schedule.

**THE BALANCE BETWEEN PHYSICAL ACTIVITY AND REST**

Just as rest is vital to recovery, it's important to find a balance between exercise and rest. Listen to your body and allow adequate time for recovery, especially after intense exercise, to avoid physical and mental exhaustion.

Incorporating physical activities into your routine is an investment in your mental, emotional and physical health, contributing to greater productivity and general well-being. By taking care of your body, you will be equipped to face mental challenges with greater clarity, focus, and creativity.

In the next chapter, "**MINDFULNESS AND FOCUS**," we will explore how practicing mindfulness can further enhance your ability to concentrate and mental efficiency. Ready to dive into mindfulness techniques that can transform your productivity? Let's move forward, exploring the deep connection between mind and body in the search for a more balanced and productive life.

# MINDFULNESS AND FOCUS

The practice of mindfulness has gained prominence as a powerful tool for improving focus, mental clarity and productivity. By teaching us to be present and aware in the current moment, without judgment, mindfulness can help us navigate the daily chaos with greater serenity and efficiency. This chapter explores how integrating mindfulness into your daily life can improve your ability to concentrate and, as a result, increase your productivity.

## UNDERSTANDING MINDFULNESS

Mindfulness is the practice of intentionally paying attention to the present moment, observing thoughts, feelings and sensations without judgment. This practice helps develop greater awareness of our patterns of thought and behavior, allowing us to respond to situations with greater calm and clarity, rather than reacting automatically.

## BENEFITS OF MINDFULNESS FOR PRODUCTIVITY

- **Reduced stress and anxiety** : By practicing mindfulness, you learn to better deal with stress and anxiety, which can lead to a calmer and more productive work environment.

- **Improved concentration** : Mindfulness increases the ability to stay focused on a task for longer, reducing the tendency to distraction.

- **Increased creativity** : Regular mindfulness practice can improve creativity, offering new perspectives and innovative solutions to complex problems.

## MINDFULNESS PRACTICES TO INTEGRATE INTO YOUR DAY

- **Daily meditation** : Set aside time each day to meditate, starting with short sessions of 5 to 10 minutes and gradually increasing as you feel comfortable.

- **Mindful breathing** : When you feel overwhelmed or distracted, take a break to focus on your breathing. A few minutes of deep breathing can help reset your mind and improve focus.

**- Mindfulness in everyday tasks** : Practice being fully present in simple daily activities, such as eating, walking or bathing, noticing all the sensations involved in these activities.

## DEVELOPING A SUSTAINABLE PRACTICE

Success in practicing mindfulness depends on regularity and commitment. It can be helpful to set reminders or incorporate mindfulness sessions into your daily routine to ensure consistency. Remember, the goal is not to empty your mind, but to observe what appears without judgment.

Adopting mindfulness can transform not only your productivity, but also your quality of life, promoting greater inner peace and satisfaction. By practicing mindfulness, you will develop a greater awareness of yourself and your surroundings, allowing you to approach tasks and challenges with a new perspective.

In the next chapter, "**OPTIMIZED WORK ENVIRONMENT**", we will discuss how to create a workspace that promotes concentration and productivity. Ready to shape your environment in ways that support your mindfulness and concentration efforts? Let's move forward, exploring how the space around us can profoundly influence our performance and well-being.

# OPTIMIZED WORK ENVIRONMENT

The configuration of our work environment can have a significant impact on our productivity and mental well-being. A well-organized, ergonomic and stimulating space not only promotes concentration and efficiency, but can also positively influence our mood and motivation. In this chapter, we'll explore how to optimize your work environment to promote focus and productivity, taking into account both physical and psychological aspects of the space.

**ELEMENTS OF A PRODUCTIVE WORK ENVIRONMENT**

- **Organized and distraction-free space** : A cluttered workspace can be distracting and even increase stress levels. Take time to organize your work area, keeping only what you need in view.

- **Adequate lighting** : Natural light is ideal as it can improve mood and energy. If natural light is not an option, choose lighting that mimics daylight and minimizes eye strain.

- **Ergonomics** : Invest in ergonomic furniture — such as chairs with adequate support and height-adjustable desks — to promote correct posture and reduce the risk of discomfort or injury.

- **Personalization** : Add personal elements that increase your motivation or happiness, such as plants, photos or a piece of art. A touch of personalization can make a space more welcoming and inspiring.

- **Dedicated zones** : If possible, create separate areas for different types of work, such as a workstation for tasks that require concentration and a separate space for reading or meetings.

**PROMOTING AN ENVIRONMENT OF FOCUS**

In addition to physically setting up your space, consider practices that help maintain a focused work environment:

- **Minimize interruptions** : Inform colleagues and family of your focused work hours and consider using visual cues, such as a "do not disturb" sign, when necessary.

- **Noise management** : If noise is distracting, use noise-cancelling headphones or listen to white music or nature sounds to drown out sound interruptions.

- **Take strategic breaks** : Use areas outside your immediate workspace to take short breaks, which can help avoid fatigue and maintain productivity throughout the day.

## REASSESSMENT AND ADJUSTMENT

The ideal work environment is one that evolves with your needs. Make regular assessments of your space and be open to making adjustments. Small changes, like rearranging your desk or updating your decor, can re-energize your space and inspire new motivation.

Creating an optimized work environment is a fundamental step towards achieving and maintaining productivity. By investing time and effort into perfecting your space, you will be laying the foundation for more effective and satisfactory performance.

Next chapter, "**CONSTANT LEARNING AND GROWTH**", we will explore how a growth mindset and dedication to continuous learning are essential for improving productivity and personal fulfillment. Ready to continue developing and reach new levels of success? Let's move forward, nurturing a culture of constant learning and adaptation.

# CONSTANT LEARNING AND GROWTH

A commitment to constant learning and growth is essential not only for personal productivity, but also for satisfaction and fulfillment in life and career. Maintaining a growth mindset — the belief that your skills and intelligence can be developed with effort, strategies, and help from others — is crucial to overcoming challenges and achieving goals. In this chapter, we'll explore how cultivating a culture of constant learning and adaptability can boost your productivity and enrich your personal and professional journey.

## THE IMPORTANCE OF CONTINUOUS LEARNING

- **Adaptability** : In a world that is always changing, the ability to learn and adapt is essential. Continuous learning allows you to stay relevant in your field and be prepared for new challenges.

- **Problem solving** : Exposure to new ideas and knowledge can improve your ability to think critically and creatively, essential for solving complex problems.

- **Motivation and engagement** : Setting learning goals and achieving them can be deeply satisfying, increasing your motivation and engagement both at work and in your personal life.

## STRATEGIES TO FOSTER CONTINUOUS LEARNING

- **Set learning objectives** : Be specific about what you want to learn and why. Setting clear goals can help you stay focused and motivated.

- **Diversify your learning sources** : Explore a wide range of resources such as books, podcasts, online courses, workshops and webinars. This can enrich your learning experience and offer different perspectives on a subject.

- **Learn by doing** : The practical application of knowledge is one of the most effective ways to learn. Look for opportunities to practice new skills, whether on personal projects, at work or in volunteer activities.

**- Create a learning network** : Connect with others who are interested in learning and growing. This may include mentors, co-workers, or study groups. Learning in a community can provide additional support and enrich your learning journey.

**- Reflect and adjust** : Set aside time regularly to reflect on what you've learned and how you can apply that knowledge. Be open to adjusting your learning plans based on your experiences and feedback.

Taking a proactive approach to constant learning and growth not only increases your productivity but also enriches your life with new skills, ideas, and experiences. By remaining curious and committed to personal development, you will be well equipped to face future challenges and seize the opportunities that arise.

In the next chapter, "**RESILIENCE AND STRESS MANAGEMENT**," we'll explore how developing resilience and managing stress effectively are crucial skills for maintaining productivity and well-being in the face of challenges and uncertainty. Ready to strengthen your ability to deal with pressure and adapt to adversity? Let us move forward, cultivating a resilient mind and spirit, ready for any challenge that may arise.

# RESILIENCE AND STRESS MANAGEMENT

Resilience is the ability to recover quickly from difficulties; It is what allows us to face challenges, adapt to changes and continue despite setbacks. Effective stress management, in turn, is fundamental to maintaining resilience and productivity. This chapter focuses on strategies for building resilience and managing stress in healthy ways, allowing you to navigate challenges with greater balance and effectiveness.

## DEVELOPING RESILIENCE

Resilience is not an innate characteristic, but rather a skill that can be developed and strengthened over time. Here are some strategies to build your resilience:

- **Cultivate a positive mindset** : See challenges as opportunities for learning and growth. Maintaining a positive outlook helps to mitigate the effects of stress and view adversity in a more manageable way.

- **Establish connections** : Strengthening relationships with friends, family and colleagues can offer emotional and practical support during difficult times. A sense of belonging is a crucial component of resilience.

- **Accept that change is part of life** : Recognizing and accepting that changes and challenges are inevitable helps you more easily adjust your expectations and adapt to new realities.

- **Take decisive action** : Instead of shutting down when faced with problems, take proactive steps to resolve them. Feeling in control of your actions can increase your sense of personal effectiveness.

## EFFECTIVE STRESS MANAGEMENT

Managing stress effectively is crucial to maintaining mental and physical health, as well as productivity. Some techniques include:

- **Relaxation techniques** : Practices such as meditation, deep breathing and yoga can help reduce tension and promote calm.

**- Regular exercise** : Physical activity is a powerful tool for combating stress, releasing endorphins that improve mood and reduce anxiety.

**- Time management** : Organizing your tasks and commitments efficiently can help reduce stress related to work overload. Learn to say no to demands that exceed your capacity.

**- Take care of yourself** : Nourishing your body with healthy foods, ensuring quality sleep, and dedicating time to hobbies and personal interests are essential for recovering from stress.

By cultivating resilience and effectively managing stress, you equip yourself to face challenges with confidence and maintain your productivity, even under pressure. These skills not only help you navigate the ups and downs of professional and personal life, but also contribute to your overall well-being and satisfaction.

In the next chapter, "**TOOLS AND APPS FOR PRODUCTIVITY**," we'll dive into the digital world to explore how the right tools and apps can optimize your time management, organization, and effectiveness at work. Ready to discover how technology can be your ally in building a more productive and less stressful life? Let us move forward, equipping ourselves with the best tools to face our daily challenges.

# TOOLS AND APPS FOR PRODUCTIVITY

In today's fast-paced world, productivity tools and applications can be valuable allies in managing our time, organizing tasks and optimizing work. With so many options available, it can be a challenge to identify which ones will best suit your needs. This chapter focuses on highlighting some of the most effective tools and apps for improving your productivity, helping you navigate your options with greater confidence.

## TASK MANAGEMENT APPS

- **Todoist** : With a simple and intuitive interface, Todoist allows you to create tasks and sub-tasks , set priorities and deadlines, and organize your tasks into projects.

- **Asana** : Excellent for teamwork, Asana makes it easy to track project progress, assign tasks and set deadlines in a visual and collaborative interface.

## TIME MANAGEMENT TOOLS

- **Toggl** : Ideal for time tracking, Toggl helps you monitor how much time you spend on different tasks and projects, providing insights into your efficiency.

- **Pomodone** : Integrating the Pomodoro Technique with the most popular task management tools, Pomodone is perfect for those looking to improve focus and time management.

## NOTE-TAKING AND ORGANIZATION APPS

- **Evernote** : A powerful solution for taking notes, organizing documents and capturing ideas in multiple formats, Evernote is a true digital archive that syncs across all your devices.

- **Notion** : Offering a unique combination of notes, tasks, databases, and wikis, Notion is extremely flexible, adapting to a wide variety of organization and productivity needs.

## FOCUSING AND DISTRACTION BLOCKING TOOLS

- **Freedom** : Allows you to block distracting websites and apps on all your devices, helping you stay focused on tasks that require attention.

- **Cold Turkey** : A robust tool that blocks digital distractions, offering customizable options to meet your focus needs.

## TIPS FOR CHOOSING THE RIGHT TOOLS

- **Identify your needs** : Before choosing a tool, consider which aspects of your productivity need the most support – whether it's task management, organization, time tracking, or blocking distractions.

- **Try before you commit** : Many tools offer free versions or trial periods. Take advantage of these opportunities to try things out before making a financial commitment.

- **Simplicity is key** : Tools that are too complicated can end up consuming more time than they save. Look for apps with intuitive interfaces and smooth learning curves.

Equipped with the right tools, you are now prepared to tackle your daily tasks with greater efficiency and effectiveness. Remember that the key to productivity isn't just in the tools you use, but in how you use them to support your work processes and habits.

In the next chapter, "**DELEGATION AND TEAMWORK**", we will explore how the art of delegating tasks and collaborating effectively can multiply your efforts and lead to even more productive results. Ready to improve your teamwork and leadership skills to achieve shared goals? Let's move forward, exploring how we can achieve more together.

# DELEGATION AND TEAMWORK

The ability to delegate tasks efficiently and work well as a team is crucial to increasing productivity and achieving significant results. However, many professionals and leaders struggle with delegation, whether out of fear of losing control or uncertainty about the team's capabilities. This chapter is dedicated to demystifying the delegation process and highlighting the importance of collaborative teamwork for overall success and productivity.

**THE ART OF DELEGATION**

Delegating does not simply mean passing tasks on to someone else; It's a strategic process that involves identifying the right tasks to delegate, choosing the right people for them, and communicating your expectations clearly. Here are some tips for delegating effectively:

- **Identify delegable tasks** : Evaluate your tasks and determine which ones can be delegated. Consider delegating tasks that are repetitive, that can be better performed by someone with specific skills, or that offer growth opportunities for team members.

- **Choose the right person** : Consider your team's skills and interests when delegating tasks. Assigning tasks that align with team members' strengths and development goals can increase motivation and effectiveness.

- **Communicate clear expectations** : Provide clear instructions, deadlines, and required resources. Establishing clear expectations from the start can avoid misunderstandings and ensure the desired results are achieved.

- **Provide support and feedback** : Be available to answer questions and offer support as needed. Regular feedback, both positive and constructive, is essential for team growth and improvement.

## BUILDING A PRODUCTIVE TEAM

Productive teamwork goes beyond effective delegation. It involves building an environment where collaboration, communication and trust flourish. Here are some strategies to strengthen your team:

- **Promote open communication** : Encourage a culture of open and honest communication where everyone feels comfortable sharing ideas and concerns.

- **Establish clear, shared goals** : Make sure everyone on the team understands the common goals and how their individual tasks contribute to achieving them.

- **Celebrate successes and learn from mistakes** : Recognize and celebrate team achievements. View mistakes as opportunities for collective learning rather than reasons for blame.

- **Foster mutual trust and respect** : Build trusting relationships within the team, respecting differences and valuing each person's contributions.

Mastering the art of delegation and cultivating a collaborative teamwork environment are key steps to improving productivity and achieving sustainable success. By implementing these strategies, you will not only optimize your team's work, but also promote a more motivating and engaged environment.

In the next chapter, **"THE POWER OF 'NO,'"** we'll explore how learning to say no can be a crucial strategy for staying focused on your priorities and managing your time and resources more effectively. Ready to discover how assertiveness can be a valuable tool on your journey to greater productivity? Let's move forward, mastering the art of establishing healthy limits.

# THE POWER OF "NO"

The ability to say "no" is one of the most underrated skills in the pursuit of productivity and work-life balance. Learning to turn down requests, opportunities, or demands that don't align with your priorities or goals can free up significant time and energy for what really matters. This chapter explores how to use the power of "no" to focus on your priorities, manage your time better, and live according to your values.

## UNDERSTANDING THE IMPORTANCE OF SAYING "NO"

Saying "no" can be challenging, especially in cultures that value availability and collaboration. However, every "yes" to something that is less important means less time and energy for your true priorities. Here are some reasons why saying "no" is vital:

- **Protects your time** : Your time is a limited resource. Saying "no" helps protect you, ensuring that you can focus on activities that truly add value to your life and work.

- **Reduces stress** : Taking on more than you can handle is a recipe for stress. Learning to say "no" can prevent burnout and promote well-being.

- **Promotes focus** : By turning down secondary tasks or projects, you can focus your energy on tasks that advance your goals.

## HOW TO SAY "NO" EFFECTIVELY

Saying "no" takes practice and skill. Here are some tips for doing this respectfully and effectively:

- **Be direct but kind** : You don't need to give a long explanation. A simple "Unfortunately, I can't commit to this at the moment" is usually enough.

- **Offer alternatives** : If possible, offer alternatives or suggest someone else who can help. This shows that you are still willing to help, even if you can't fulfill the request.

- **Know your priorities** : Being clear about your priorities makes it easier to decide what to refuse. If something doesn't align with your current goals, it's a clear candidate for a "no."

- **Practice** : Like any skill, saying "no" gets easier with practice. Start with small requests and work your way up until you feel more comfortable turning down larger commitments.

## THE POSITIVE IMPACT OF SAYING "NO"

Far from being a sign of refusal or limitation, learning to say "no" is an act of affirming your values and priorities. It allows you to dedicate more of your time, attention and resources to the things that are truly important, resulting in greater satisfaction and productivity.

Mastering the art of saying "no" is essential to effectively managing your time and energy, allowing you to focus on the activities that matter most. As you practice and become more comfortable with this skill, you will find more balance and control over your life and work.

In the next chapter, "**PRODUCTIVITY AND LIFE BALANCE**," we'll explore how finding a healthy balance between work, play, and personal life is crucial to maintaining sustainable productivity and overall well-being. Ready to learn strategies to create a more balanced and fulfilled life? Let's move forward, discovering how to harmoniously integrate all facets of your life.

# PRODUCTIVITY AND LIFE BALANCE

Finding a healthy balance between work, leisure and personal life is key to sustaining long-term productivity and maintaining well-being. The challenge of balancing these elements can seem daunting in a world that often values constant busyness as a sign of success. This chapter addresses the importance of seeking a life balance that not only preserves your health and happiness, but also enhances your productivity.

## THE IMPORTANCE OF LIFE BALANCE

A healthy life balance reduces the risk of burnout, increases overall satisfaction, and promotes a fuller, richer life. When we dedicate adequate time to rest, leisure and relationships, our ability to work effectively and creatively is significantly improved.

## STRATEGIES FOR ACHIEVING LIFE BALANCE

- **Establish clear boundaries** : Set clear boundaries between work and personal life. This can include specific times when work starts and ends, as well as periods dedicated to family, friends, and hobbies.

- **Prioritize quality time** : Focus on the quality of time spent, not just quantity. This means being present during time with loved ones or while participating in leisure activities, without the distractions of work.

- **Learn to say "no"** : As discussed in the previous chapter, knowing how to refuse commitments or tasks that don't align with your priorities is crucial to maintaining a healthy balance.

- **Take care of your health** : Include regular physical activity, healthy eating and adequate sleep in your routine. Physical and mental health are fundamental to maintaining the energy and focus necessary for productivity.

- **Flexibility and adaptation** : Be flexible and willing to adjust your approach to life balance as your circumstances change. The perfect balance for you may vary over time and at different stages of life.

**INTEGRATING PRODUCTIVITY AND LIFE BALANCE**

Integrating productivity and life balance means recognizing that time dedicated to rest and leisure is not wasted time, but an essential part of the creative and productive process. By allowing you to recharge, these moments contribute to your ability to generate ideas, solve problems, and maintain motivation.

Achieving a satisfactory life balance is an ongoing process of self-discovery and adjustment. By implementing strategies that promote this balance, you will be better equipped to enjoy a more productive and fulfilled life.

In the next chapter, "**EVALUATING YOUR PRODUCTIVITY**," we'll focus on methods for measuring and evaluating your productivity, allowing you to make adjustments as needed to maintain the ideal work-life balance. Ready to further refine your approach to productivity? Let us move forward, equipping ourselves with the tools to measure our success and make continuous improvements.

# EVALUATING YOUR PRODUCTIVITY

Assessing your productivity is essential to understanding how you are spending your time and energy, and whether your work and life balance strategies are effectively contributing to your goals. This evaluation process allows you to identify areas for improvement and make necessary adjustments to optimize your efficiency. In this chapter, we'll explore methods and tools for measuring your productivity and analyzing your performance, facilitating a continuous cycle of growth and improvement.

**WHY EVALUATE YOUR PRODUCTIVITY?**

Regular productivity assessment helps to:

- **Identify productive and distracting patterns** : Understand when and where you are most productive, in addition to which activities or habits are harming your performance.

- **Adjust strategies and methods** : Making changes based on concrete data about what works well and what doesn't allows you to improve your work and time management techniques.

- **Define and refine objectives** : Assessing progress against your goals can motivate and guide adjustments to your action plans.

**METHODS TO ASSESS YOUR PRODUCTIVITY**

- **Time tracking** : Use time tracking apps or tools to record how much time you spend on different activities. Analyze the data to identify where you can optimize your time.

- **Weekly/monthly reviews** : Take time regularly to review what you have achieved in relation to your goals. Ask yourself what was successful and what could be improved.

- **Third-party feedback** : Getting feedback from colleagues, supervisors, or mentors can offer an outside perspective on your productivity and areas for development.

- **Goal-based self-assessment** : Set clear success criteria for your tasks and projects. When completing a task, evaluate whether these criteria were met and what could be improved.

## USEFUL TOOLS FOR PRODUCTIVITY ASSESSMENT

- **Toggl** , **RescueTime** , **Clockify** : Time tracking apps that give you detailed insights into how you spend your day.

- **Notion** , **Evernote** : Organization platforms that can be used to record progress, reflections and action plans.

## IMPLEMENTING IMPROVEMENTS

After evaluating your productivity, implement improvements incrementally. Focus on one or two areas of adjustment at a time to avoid overload. Celebrate small victories and progress as this serves as motivation to continue improving your productivity.

Regularly assessing your productivity is a crucial step towards ongoing personal and professional development. With the right tools and methods, you can turn insights into action, driving significant improvements in your efficiency and well-being.

In the next chapter, "**AVOIDING PROCRASTINATION**," we'll dive into strategies for overcoming one of the biggest obstacles to productivity. Ready to face procrastination head-on and pave the way for unprecedented efficiency? Let's move forward, equipping ourselves with techniques to overcome procrastination and achieve our goals.

# AVOIDING PROCRASTINATION

Procrastination is a common barrier many face on their journey to becoming more productive. The tendency to put off tasks can lead to a cycle of stress, guilt and even lower self-esteem. However, with effective strategies and a change in mindset, it is possible to overcome procrastination and cultivate more productive habits. This chapter covers techniques and approaches for avoiding procrastination, allowing you to accomplish more and reach your goals with confidence.

## UNDERSTANDING PROCRASTINATION

To combat procrastination, it is crucial to understand its causes. Generally, procrastination is driven by fear of failure, perfectionism, lack of clarity, or insufficient motivation. Recognizing the underlying reasons can help create specific strategies to overcome them.

## STRATEGIES TO AVOID PROCRASTINATION

- **Break down large tasks** : Big projects can seem overwhelming. Break them down into smaller, more manageable tasks to reduce resistance to getting started.

- **Set clear deadlines** : Set realistic deadlines for yourself, even for projects that don't have one. Deadlines create a sense of urgency that can drive action.

- **Change the environment** : Modify your work environment to reduce distractions. An organized space dedicated to work can improve focus.

- **Rewards and consequences** : Establish rewards for completing tasks and consequences for procrastinating. This can help create additional motivation to take action.

- **Five-minute technique** : Commit to working on a task for at least five minutes. Often, getting started is the hardest part, and once you start, you're more likely to keep going.

- **Mindfulness and self-awareness** : Practice mindfulness

to increase awareness of your procrastination patterns. Actively questioning why you are procrastinating can help you identify solutions.

**- Reframe your mindset** : Change your internal dialogue from "I have to do this" to "I choose to do this." This can help transform the perception of the task from a burden to an active choice.

Overcoming procrastination is a gradual process that requires patience, understanding and persistence. By applying these strategies, you will develop a more proactive approach to work and life, paving the way for greater productivity and satisfaction.

In the next chapter, "**FINANCIAL PLANNING AND PRODUCTIVITY**," we will explore how effective financial management can free up energy and attention for more productive tasks. Ready to understand the connection between your financial health and your productivity? Let's move forward, discovering how financial peace of mind can be a powerful catalyst for your performance.

# FINANCIAL PLANNING AND PRODUCTIVITY

Effective management of personal and business finances plays a crucial role in productivity. Financial worries can be a significant source of stress and distraction, negatively impacting the ability to concentrate and accomplish tasks effectively. This chapter explores how strategic financial planning can not only provide financial security, but also free up your mental energy and resources to focus on productive activities, advancing your personal and professional goals.

## THE CONNECTION BETWEEN FINANCIAL HEALTH AND PRODUCTIVITY

- **Reduces stress** : Financial worries are one of the main causes of stress. Solid financial planning reduces this source of anxiety, allowing you to focus more on important tasks.

- **Improves decision making** : The financial peace of mind provided by effective planning improves the ability to make rational and well-informed decisions in all areas of life.

- **Frees up time and energy** : Managing financial crises consumes time and energy that could be better used in productive and creative activities.

## STRATEGIES FOR EFFICIENT FINANCIAL PLANNING

- **Establish a budget** : Creating and following a budget helps you monitor expenses, control superfluous spending and prioritize investment in resources that contribute to your goals.

- **Build an emergency fund** : Having an emergency fund can prevent financial stress caused by unforeseen events, ensuring you can stay focused on your long-term goals.

- **Invest in your growth** : Allocate resources for your education and professional development. Investing in skills and knowledge can open doors to new opportunities and increase your productivity and earning potential.

- **Automate your finances** : Use financial tools and services to automate payments and transfers. This can save time and reduce worry about deadlines and payments.

- **Regularly review your finances** : As with evaluating productivity, periodic reviews of your financial situation are essential to adjust plans and strategies as necessary.

Integrating financial planning into your productivity approach is a powerful strategy for achieving both financial stability and life goals. By taking the time and effort to proactively manage your finances, you create an environment conducive to personal and professional growth.

In the next chapter, "**FUTURE OF PRODUCTIVITY**", we will look at emerging trends and the future of work and personal productivity. Ready to explore how innovations and social changes can influence your efficiency and approach to work? Let's move forward, anticipating the future and preparing to adapt our productivity strategies to a world in constant evolution.

# FUTURE OF PRODUCTIVITY

As we move into the 21st century, the future of productivity appears to lie at the intersection of technological innovation, changes in work practices, and an increasing emphasis on well-being and life balance. This chapter explores emerging trends and how they could shape the future of work and personal productivity, offering insights into how we can prepare for and adapt to these changes to maintain and improve our efficiency.

**EMERGING TRENDS IN PRODUCTIVITY**

- **Remote and flexible work** : The global pandemic has accelerated the adoption of remote work, showing that many tasks can be performed outside of a traditional office environment. This trend is set to continue, with more companies offering flexible work options, recognizing the importance of work-life balance for productivity.

- **Automation and artificial intelligence (AI)** : AI and automation tools are becoming increasingly sophisticated, capable of taking over repetitive tasks and freeing humans to focus on creative and strategic work. Learning to integrate these tools into your daily workflow will be key to increasing productivity.

- **Continuous learning and skill development** : As the job market evolves, the ability to adapt and learn new skills quickly will become even more critical. Future productivity will depend not just on what we know, but on how quickly we can learn and apply new knowledge.

- **Well-being and conscious productivity** : There is a growing awareness of the importance of physical and mental well-being in productivity. In the future, we hope to see a more holistic approach to productivity, one that balances efficiency with health and personal satisfaction.

**PREPARING FOR THE FUTURE**

- **Flexibility and adaptation** : Develop the ability to quickly adapt to new technologies and working methods. Flexibility will be one of the most valuable skills in the future of work.

- **Focus on continuous learning** : Commit to ongoing personal and professional development. Explore online learning resources and attend trainings and workshops to keep your skills up to date.

- **Integration of well-being into your work routine** : Adopt practices that promote a healthy lifestyle, such as regular breaks, physical exercise and mindfulness techniques. Remember that sustainable productivity requires a healthy mind and body.

- **Strategic use of technology** : Keep an eye on technological innovations and evaluate how they can be integrated into your work to increase efficiency. However, be critical and conscious to avoid tool overload.

The future of productivity is bright and full of opportunities for those willing to adapt and grow. By staying informed about emerging trends and developing the skills you need to navigate the future of work, you'll be well positioned to seize the opportunities these changes will bring.

In the next chapter, "**CREATING YOUR PERSONAL PRODUCTIVITY FORMULA**," we'll consolidate the insights and strategies discussed so far, helping you develop a personalized plan that aligns with your goals, lifestyle, and emerging trends. Ready to create your own productivity formula? Let us move forward, equipping ourselves for a productive and satisfying future.

# CREATING YOUR PERSONAL PRODUCTIVITY FORMULA

Productivity is not a one-size-fits-all solution. Each person has their own goals, lifestyles, preferences and challenges. Therefore, it is essential to create a personal productivity formula that respects your individuality and makes the most of your strengths. This chapter is dedicated to helping you develop a personalized productivity plan, combining the strategies discussed previously with your unique needs and circumstances.

## STEPS TO DEVELOP YOUR PERSONAL PRODUCTIVITY FORMULA

- **Self-Assessment** : Start with an honest assessment of your current work patterns, productivity habits, and areas of challenge. Identify which techniques work well for you and where you frequently encounter obstacles.

- **Define your goals and priorities** : Clarify what you want to achieve in the short, medium and long term. Understanding your priorities helps you align your productivity strategies with your broader goals.

- **Choose your tools and methods** : Based on self-assessment and your goals, select tools and methods that suit your work style. This could include specific time management techniques, productivity apps, or approaches to minimizing procrastination.

- **Integrate well-being practices** : Recognize the importance of physical and mental well-being in productivity. Incorporate healthy habits like regular exercise, mindful breaks, and a good sleep routine into your plan.

- **Establish a review system** : Create a system to regularly review your progress toward your goals and adjust your approach as needed. This may involve weekly, monthly or quarterly reviews.

- **Experiment and adjust** : Be open to experimentation. Try different strategies and see what improves your productivity. Don't be afraid to adjust or abandon methods that aren't working.

## TIPS FOR MAINTAINING YOUR PRODUCTIVITY FORMULA

- **Flexibility** : Your productivity formula will evolve over time. Be flexible and adapt your approach to changes in your circumstances or goals.

- **Simplicity** : Avoid overcomplicating your system. Simplicity makes it easier to maintain consistency and reduces resistance.

- **Consistency** : Regular practice and consistency are key to transforming strategies into lasting habits.

- **Share and learn** : Share your experiences with others and be open to learning from their productivity strategies. Interacting with a community can offer new ideas and support.

Creating and refining your personal productivity formula is an ongoing process of discovery and adjustment. By taking the time to understand what works best for you, you lay a solid foundation for achieving your goals and living a fuller, more satisfying life.

In the next chapter, "**INTEGRATING PRODUCTIVITY INTO LIFE**", we will close with reflections on how to sustainably integrate productivity into all aspects of your life, aiming not only for professional success, but also for personal and general well-being. Let us move forward to consolidate our learning and apply it to a holistic vision of productivity and achievement.

# INTEGRATING PRODUCTIVITY INTO LIFE

As we come to the end of this exploratory productivity journey, it is essential to reflect on how to sustainably integrate the strategies and insights gained into all aspects of your life. Productivity is not limited to completing tasks or meeting professional goals; it is a holistic approach that encompasses personal fulfillment, well-being and satisfaction in various areas of life. This final chapter highlights the importance of balancing efficiency with well-being and offers guidance for carrying forward the lessons learned, promoting a productive and fulfilling life.

## PRODUCTIVITY AS A PHILOSOPHY OF LIFE

- **Balance is key** : True productivity is achieved when there is a healthy balance between work, leisure and self-care. Strive to maintain this balance, adjusting your practices as needed to meet the demands of different areas of your life.

- **Continuous growth** : See productivity as a path to continuous personal and professional growth. Be open to new learning and challenges that stimulate your development.

- **Sustainability** : Adopt productivity practices that are sustainable in the long term. Avoid the trap of seeking efficiency at all costs, which can lead to burnout. Prioritize methods that promote health and well-being.

## TAKING LESSONS FORWARD

- **Practice self-reflection** : Take time regularly to reflect on your productivity journey. Assess what's working, what's not, and what can be improved.

- **Adapt and evolve** : Be resilient and adaptable to changes in your personal and professional life and external circumstances. A willingness to adjust your approach can help you maintain productivity in the face of unexpected challenges.

- **Share your knowledge** : Share your productivity experiences and learnings with others. Teaching and mentoring can reinforce your own understanding and inspire those around you.

The journey to improving productivity is ongoing and deeply personal. By applying the principles and strategies discussed in this book to your life, you establish a solid foundation for achieving not only external success, but also internal satisfaction and well-being.

Remember, the most meaningful productivity is the one that allows you to live according to your values, achieve your dreams, and contribute positively to the world around you. May this book serve as a guide on your journey to a more productive and fulfilled life.

Thank you for following this far. The path ahead is yours to walk, with the tools and insights you've gathered. Move forward with confidence, flexibility, and an open mind to the endless possibilities your personalized productivity can unlock.

As we turn the final page of this journey together, I sincerely hope that the learnings shared here have touched your heart and sparked new perspectives. If this book has brought you any value, I kindly ask that you take a few moments to leave a review on Amazon. Your words not only help me grow and hone my craft, but they also guide other readers in their quests for knowledge and inspiration. Your opinion is a valuable gift, both for me and for the community of readers looking for stories that transform. I sincerely thank you for sharing this journey with me and I hope we can meet again in the pages of a new adventure.

# REGINALDO OSNILDO

# REGINALDO OSNILDO

Hello, I'm Reginaldo Osnildo, author and innovator in the fields of sales, technology, and communication strategies. My background spans from the academic setting, as a professor and researcher at the University of Southern Santa Catarina, to hands-on strategy development at the Catarinense Radio Group. With a PhD in sales narratives and digital convergence, and a Master's in storytelling and social imaginary, I offer my readers a unique blend of theory and practice. My aim is to deliver knowledge in a simple, practical, and didactic language, encouraging direct application in one's personal and professional life.

Yours sincerely

**Reginaldo Osnildo**

**+55 48 991913865**

**reginaldoosnildo@gmail.com**

www.ingramcontent.com/pod-product-compliance
Lightning Source LLC
Chambersburg PA
CBHW070350230526
45471CB00006B/2498